Smithsonian

Exploring
the
New Jersey
Colony

by Barbara Krasner

CAPSTONE PRESS
a capstone imprint

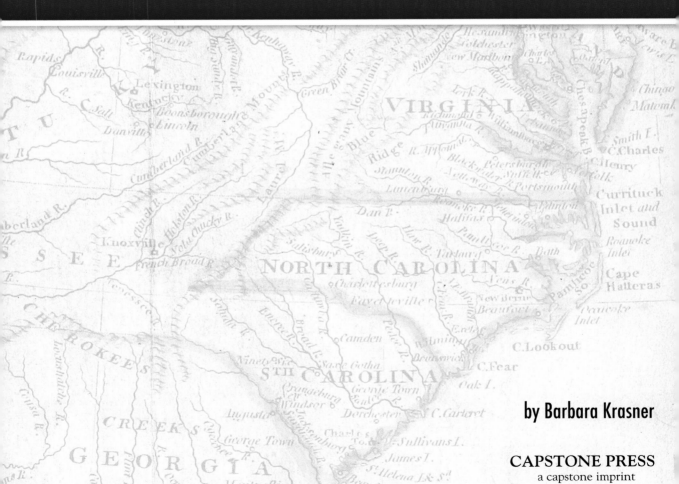

Smithsonian books are published by Capstone Press,
1710 Roe Crest Drive, North Mankato, Minnesota 56003
www.capstonepub.com

Library of Congress Cataloging-in-Publication Data
Names: Krasner, Barbara, author.
Title: Exploring the New Jersey Colony / by Barbara Krasner.
Description: North Mankato, Minnesota: Capstone Press, 2017. | Series: Smithsonian. Exploring the 13
colonies | Includes bibliographical references and index.
Identifiers: LCCN 2016013014| ISBN 9781515722359 (library binding) | ISBN 9781515722489 (pbk.) |
ISBN 9781515722618 (ebook (pdf))
Subjects: LCSH: New Jersey—History—Colonial period, ca. 1600–1775—Juvenile literature. | New
Jersey—History—Revolution, 1775–1783—Juvenile literature.
Classification: LCC F137 K73 2017 | DDC 974.9/02—dc23
LC record available at http://lccn.loc.gov/2016013014

Editorial Credits
Jennifer Huston, editor; Richard Parker, designer; Eric Gohl, media researcher;
Kathy McColley, production specialist

Our very special thanks to Stephen Binns at the Smithsonian Center for Learning and Digital Access for
his curatorial review. Capstone would also like to thank Kealy Gordon, Smithsonian Institution Product
Development Manager, and the following at Smithsonian Enterprises: Christopher A. Liedel, President;
Carol LeBlanc, Senior Vice President; Brigid Ferraro, Vice President; Ellen Nanney, Licensing Manager.

Photo Credits
Alamy: Everett Collection Inc., 38, Niday Picture Library, 37; Bridgeman Images: John H. Morgan,
Dick S. Ramsay Fund, Museum Collection Fund/Brooklyn Museum of Art, New York, USA, 25, Peter
Newark American Pictures/Private Collection, 7; Capstone: 4; Courtesy of Army Art Collection, U.S.
Army Center of Military History: 32; Courtesy of The Historical Society of Pennsylvania: 11; Getty
Images: Bettmann, 21, MyLoupe, 8, Stringer/MPI, 36; Granger, NYC: 10, 13, 26; Library of Congress: 16,
17, 20, 41; New Jersey State Archives/Department of State: 27; New York Public Library: 12, 24, 28, 39;
North Wind Picture Archives: cover, 5, 9, 15, 18, 19, 22, 23, 29, 30, 31, 33, 34, 35, 40

Design Elements: Shutterstock

Printed and bound in the USA.
009669F16

Table of Contents

Introduction:
The 13 Colonies

In 1492 Christopher Columbus sailed westward from Spain in hopes of finding a shortcut to eastern Asia. He did not know that two huge continents—North and South America—stood in the way.

This "New World" presented adventure and opportunities for European explorers. Henry Hudson explored the Atlantic coast in 1609 for the Dutch East India Company, a trading company. Reports of his findings interested his employers. They liked the idea of trading with the Native Americans. Trade rather than settlements was their goal. But soon the Spanish, French, Dutch, and British were competing to claim land and start settlements, or **colonies**, in the New World.

The New Jersey Colony was part of the Middle Colonies region.

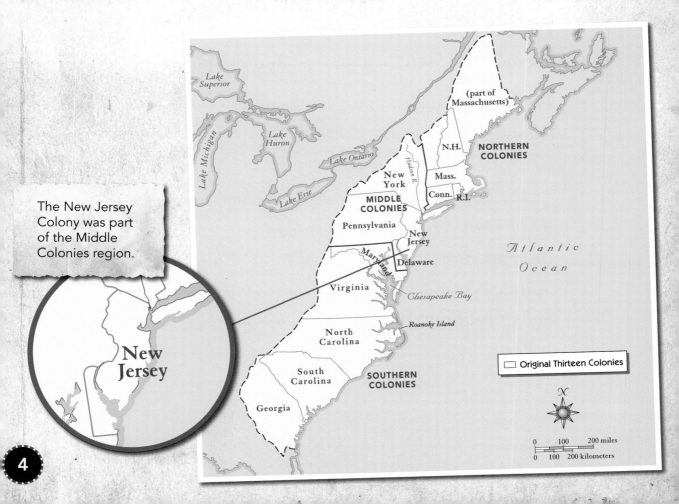

Beginning with explorer John Cabot's voyage in 1497, England claimed much of the land along North America's eastern coast. However, it would take more than 100 years for them to colonize the area. Virginia, the first English colony, was founded in 1607. In 1660 the Dutch settled the first permanent village in what is now New Jersey.

Food shortages, crowded conditions, and lack of religious freedom were some of the reasons that people left Europe to live in America. Whatever the reason, these **immigrants** braved a long journey across the Atlantic Ocean. Then they faced hard lives in a land that was new and strange to them.

colony—a place that is settled by people from another country and is controlled by that country

immigrant—someone who settles permanently in another country

The 13 Colonies can be grouped into three geographic areas: the Northern Colonies, the Middle Colonies, and the Southern Colonies. The cold weather and rocky soil of the Northern Colonies limited the types of crops that could be grown there. But the tall trees in the region were excellent for shipbuilding and producing lumber and maple syrup. The Middle Colonies became known as the "breadbasket" of the colonies because the land was good for growing wheat and other grains. The Southern Colonies offered the warmest climate and longest growing season. In the South, large farms, or **plantations**, developed for growing profitable crops, such as tobacco, cotton, rice, and **indigo**. However, the heat could be unbearable and often caused disease.

The 13 Colonies were all subjects of England, and all sent their products to the home country, but they also shared products with each other. For example, the Northern Colonies imported fruits and vegetables from the Middle Colonies. More than a century after their founding, all 13 banded together in their fight for independence from England. In this fight New Jersey would play a unique role.

The Original 13 Colonies
The first permanent European settlement in each colony:

Colony	Year	Colony	Year
Virginia	1607	Delaware	1638
Massachusetts	1620	Pennsylvania	1643
New Hampshire	1623	North Carolina	1653
New York	1624	New Jersey	1660
Connecticut	1633	South Carolina	1670
Maryland	1634	Georgia	1733
Rhode Island	1636		

NEW JERSEY

The Middle Colonies had a lot of land that was good for growing grain.

plantation—a large farm where crops are raised by people who live there

indigo—a plant that produces a deep-blue dye

Chapter 1:
New Jersey's Original People

When Europeans arrived, between 8,000 and 12,000 Lenni Lenape people were living in the land that would become New Jersey. The name "Lenni Lenape" comes from the tribe's own name for themselves. The words mean "original people." They also became known as Delawares, a name given to them by the English. The languages they spoke were part of the Algonquian language group. Men and older boys fished and hunted, sometimes for several weeks at a time. Women planted corn and took care of the children. Girls helped their mothers with the cooking. Lenni Lenapes ate corn made into cakes and **hominy**. They had no animals to help them with their work.

The frame of a wigwam was made of young trees.

The Lenni Lenape people usually settled near streams or rivers. They hollowed out logs to build canoes, which they used to travel by water.

The Lenni Lenapes lived in small groups. Their homes were called **wigwams**, which were small huts with domed roofs. Their villages were typically located on high ground near rivers and streams. They established trails and used the waterways as their highways. They spent summers near the shore to fish and gather clams, oysters, and mussels, which are all types of shellfish. They carried their catch back to their villages along the trails. In winter they lived in **longhouses**. War, natural disaster, or lack of food sometimes forced entire villages to move.

A chief ruled tribal villages. Councils of tribe members guided decisions. Although they looked to their chiefs for leadership, the people were also guided by religious beliefs. Religious customs and ceremonies shaped much of Lenni Lenape daily life.

hominy—coarsely ground corn boiled in water

wigwam—a round hut made of poles covered with bark, leaves, or animal skins

longhouse—a long, narrow house usually for members of one clan

The arrival of European settlers changed the Lenni Lenape way of life. The Lenni Lenapes influenced European ways as well. Dutch settlers brought new plants to grow, and the Dutch learned the fur trade from the Lenni Lenapes. But the two groups did not always get along. They fought two wars at Pavonia, now Jersey City, in 1643 and 1655. The second war left the area deserted.

Ordered by the governor of New Netherland, Dutch soldiers fought with and killed many of the Lenni Lenapes in 1643.

By 1700 there were fewer than 3,000 Lenni Lenapes in the New Jersey area. By 1763 that number dropped below a thousand. The trend continued. By 1800 there were fewer than 200. One reason for the decline in population was that they couldn't fight off diseases, such as **smallpox**, brought by the Europeans.

Critical Thinking with Primary Sources

In 1683 William Penn, **Quaker** and founder of Pennsylvania, wrote an account of the Delawares, or Lenni Lenapes. He described their diet, government, marriage customs, and social habits. Why do you think Penn would write about the Delawares? Are his descriptions complimentary? Support your opinion with evidence from the text.

[5]

XI. The *NATIVES* I shall confider in their *Perfons, Language, Manners, Religion* and *Government*, with my fence of their *Original*. For their *Perfons*, they are generally tall, ftreight, well-built, and of fingular Proportion; they tread ftrong and clever, and moftly walk with a lofty Chin: Of Complexion, *Black*: but by defign, as the *Gypfies* in *England*: They greafe themfelves with Bears-fat clarified, and ufing no defence againft *Sun* or *Weather*, their skins muft needs be fwarthy: Their *Eye* is little and black, not unlike a ftraight-look'd *Jew*: The thick Lip and *flat Nofe*, fo frequent with the *Eaft-Indians* and *Blacks*, are not common to them; for I have feen as comely *European*-like faces among them of both, as on your fide the Sea; and truly an *Italian Complexion* hath not much more of the *White*, and the *Nofes* of feveral of them have as much of the *Roman*.

XII. Their *Language* is lofty, yet narrow, but like the *Hebrew*; in Signification full, like *Short-hand* in writing; *one* word ferveth in the place of *three*, and the reft are fupplied by the Underftanding of the Hearer: Imperfect in their *Tenfes*, wanting in their *Moods, Participles, Adverbs, Conjunctions, Interjections*: I have made it my bufinefs to underftand it, that I might not want an Interpreter on any occafion: And I muft fay, that I know not a Language fpoken in *Europe*, that hath words of more fweetnefs or greatnefs, in *Accent* and *Emphafis*, than theirs; for Inftance, Octorockon, Rancocas, Oricton, Shakamaxon, Poquefíín, all which are names of Places, and have Grandeur in them: Of words of Sweetnefs, Anna, is *Mother*, Iffimus, *a Brother*, Netap, *Friend*, ufque oret, *very good*; pone, *Bread*, metfe, *eat*, matta, ne, hatta, *to have*, payo, *to come*; Sepaffen, Paffijon, the Names of Places; Tamane, Secane, Menanfe, Secatereus, are the Names of Perfons. If one ask them for any thing they have not, they will anfwer, matta ne hatta, which to tranflate is, *not I have*, inftead of *I have not*,

XIII. Of their *Cuftoms* and *Manners* there is much to be faid; I will begin with *Children*. So foon as they are born, they wafh them in *Water*, and while very young, and in cold Weather to chufe, they *Plunge* them in the Rivers to harden and embolden them. Having wrapt them in a Clout, they lay them on a ftraight thin Board, a little more than the length and breadth of the Child, and fwadle it faft upon the Board to make it ftraight; wherefore all *Indians* have flat Heads; and thus they carry them at their Backs. The Children will go very *young*, at *nine Moneths* commonly; they wear only a fmall Clout round their Wafte, till they are big; if *Boys*, they go a Fifhing till ripe for the Woods, which is about *Fifteen*; then they Hunt, and after having given fome Proofs of their Manhood, by a good return of *Skins*, they may *Marry*, elfe it is a fhame to think of a *Wife*. The *Girls* ftay with their Mothers, and help to hoe the Ground,

Another reason was a treaty the tribe signed in 1758 with New Jersey's British royal governor, Francis Bernard. Through this treaty New Jersey would provide space in its southern region for the Lenni Lenapes to live. This area was known as the Brotherton **Reservation**, but it ultimately failed. The remaining Lenni Lenapes were invited to join other tribes, such as the Oneidas, in Pennsylvania, New York, and Wisconsin. In 1801 the last Lenni Lenapes sold their New Jersey land. Some joined the Oneidas in northern New York while others joined the communities of European settlers.

Francis Bernard was the royal governor of New Jersey from 1758 to 1760.

Did You Know?

Lenni Lenape trails and place names are still evident in New Jersey today. These include the towns of Hackensack, Hoboken, Passaic, Raritan, and Matawan.

> *"The Dutch and Sweeds inform us that they [the native people] are greatly decreased in number to what they were when they came first into this Country: And the Indians themselves say, that two of them die to every one Christian that comes in here."*
>
> —Gabriel Thomas, a colonist in West Jersey, 1698

Bartholomew Calvin (1756?–1840)

Born around 1756 Lenni Lenape member Bartholomew Calvin lived on the Brotherton Reservation. The Scottish missionary society in Princeton, New Jersey, sent Calvin to the College of New Jersey (now Princeton University). The society was a group that did good works and taught others their **Protestant** faith.

College of New Jersey

reservation—an area of land set aside for Native Americans

Protestant—a Christian who does not belong to the Roman Catholic or the

Chapter 2:
The Founding of a Colony

In 1609 English sea captain Henry Hudson, working for the Dutch, explored the area that would become New York City and New Jersey. He then sailed 100 miles up the river that would be named for him—the Hudson. In 1624 the Dutch West India Company sent explorer Cornelius Mey to establish colonies in the region. Mey built Fort Nassau near present-day Gloucester, New Jersey. He also established a trading center for the Dutch and Lenni Lenapes, but the fort was soon abandoned.

The Dutch wanted people to settle the area, which they named New Netherland after their homeland. In 1629 the Dutch West India Company offered promises of large areas of land to anyone who agreed to bring 50 settlers. These landowners were given the title **patroon**, meaning "master." Wealthy businessman Michael Pauw accepted the offer in 1630. He obtained land on the west side of the Hudson River across from Manhattan Island, in what is now Jersey City, New Jersey. He named his land Pavonia. Pauw had trouble getting a settlement going in Pavonia, so he sold his land back to the company in 1633.

While the Dutch struggled to maintain a claim in the Hudson River Valley, the Swedish began to settle land to the south. In 1643 the New Sweden Company built Fort Nya Elfsborg along what is now the New Jersey side of the Delaware River. The fort's mission was to protect the Swedish fur trade from the Dutch and the British. But constant attacks of mosquitoes forced the soldiers to abandon the fort.

Did You Know?

Cape May, New Jersey, is named for Dutch explorer Cornelius Mey.

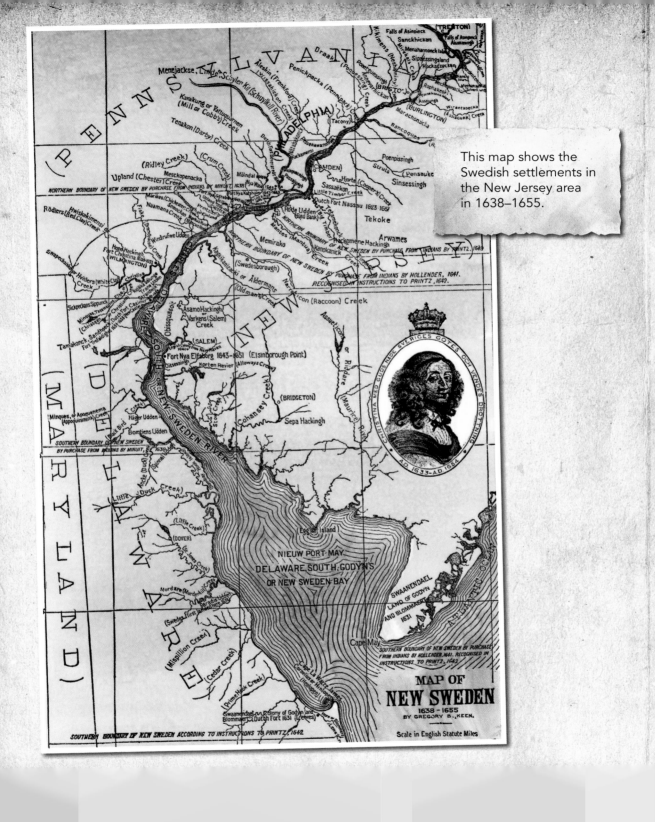

This map shows the Swedish settlements in the New Jersey area in 1638–1655.

MAP OF
NEW SWEDEN
1638 – 1655
BY GREGORY B. KEEN.

Scale in English Statute Miles

The Dutch had prior claims to the Delaware River Valley and wanted to trade there with the Lenni Lenapes. At first they allowed the Swedes to settle. But as the Swedes moved northward toward present-day Trenton, New Jersey, the Dutch were concerned that they would lose their trade and their profits. In the summer of 1655, New Netherland's governor Peter Stuyvesant led an expedition of seven ships and 600 soldiers to the Swedish settlements. Sweden tried to fight back but didn't have the military strength. Eventually Sweden gave up its claims. Of the 400 or so residents of New Sweden, many returned to Europe. Others set off for New Amsterdam (present-day New York City), the capital of New Netherland.

At that time there was no organized community in New Jersey except for Bergen. Bergen was a village founded by a German man in 1660 and later became Jersey City. But there was a colony and plenty of land. Soon the valleys of the Raritan and Hackensack Rivers had more Dutch residents than New Amsterdam.

Tielman Van Vleck, Bergen's Founder

Lawyer Tielman Van Vleck came to America in 1658 from Bremen, Germany. He asked Peter Stuyvesant, New Netherland's governor, to found Bergen, New Jersey's first permanent European village. Fearing Native American attacks, Stuyvesant refused twice. Finally in 1660 Van Vleck received permission to establish the village. In 1661 he became Bergen's first sheriff.

Bergen

Critical Thinking with Primary Sources

This map shows New Netherland's settlements along the Delaware River and Delaware Bay around 1639. It also shows some of the natural features. Do you think the people of New Sweden should have stayed? What do you think life was like along the Delaware River?

Chapter 3:
A Little Bit of Jersey

In 1664 Britain's King Charles II granted land to his brother James, the Duke of York. This land included present-day New Jersey and New York—part of the Dutch colony of New Netherland. James then granted part of the territory, the area of New Jersey, to Sir George Carteret and Lord John Berkeley. He gave them the land as a way of thanking them for their service to the crown.

But also in 1664, James sent Colonel Richard Nicolls to seize New Netherland for England. Dutch governor Peter Stuyvesant wanted to fight, but the Dutch settlers refused to support him. He gave up New Amsterdam without a struggle. Nicolls renamed it New York.

Peter Stuyvesant surrendered to the English without a fight.

Throughout England's takeover of New Netherland, communication was poor. Nicolls did not know that the Duke of York had already divided up New Jersey. When he received a request from a group of men who wanted to buy land in New Jersey, Nicolls approved. These men purchased land from local Lenni Lenape chiefs. This group of men soon moved their families from Long Island into the areas between the Raritan and Passaic Rivers.

Within two years six new towns had been established: Elizabethtown, Middletown, Shrewsbury, Woodbridge, Piscataway, and Newark. There was also the Dutch village of Bergen, granted by Carteret in 1668. While both Carteret and Berkeley were selling off their Jersey lands to **proprietors**, Nicolls was also granting land.

A Puritan woman works at her spinning wheel.

Did You Know?

New Jersey was named after the Isle of Jersey in the English Channel. George Carteret had been governor of the Isle of Jersey.

Nicolls granted land in Elizabethtown to **Puritans** from Connecticut. He gave land in Monmouth to Quakers and Baptists from New England. Another group of Puritans bought land directly from the Lenni Lenapes to establish Newark in 1666. The question of ownership became confusing and caused arguments. Settlers were told they had to pay a kind of rent, called **quitrent**. Some refused to pay.

Critical Thinking with Primary Sources

A dividing line between property owners split the New Jersey Colony into East and West sections, as shown in this 1706 map. Why do you think this happened?

Meanwhile, war broke out between England and the Netherlands in 1672. Dutch warships from the West Indies forced New York into surrender. For nearly a year, New Jersey, which was governed under the New York Colony, was back in Dutch hands. In 1674 peace was restored, and Berkeley sold half of New Jersey to two Quakers. Two years later the New Jersey Colony split into East Jersey and West Jersey, each owned by different people. Perth Amboy was the capital of East Jersey. Burlington was the capital of West Jersey.

Richard Nicolls (1624–1672)

Richard Nicolls was born in Bedfordshire, England, in 1624. He arrived in America in August 1664 at the command of James, the Duke of York. His mission was to take control of New Netherland, including the city of New Amsterdam, from the Dutch. He changed the name of the colony and city to New York in honor of the duke. As governor of the New Jersey Colony, Nicolls earned the respect of both the English and the Dutch. He returned to England after resigning as governor in 1668.

Chapter 4:
A Growing Colony

A series of splits led to arguments, physical conflict, and the division of New Jersey into East and West. England wanted to put a stop to all the overlapping land claims.

England's Queen Anne sent her cousin, Lord Cornbury, to settle the matter. In 1702 East and West Jersey came back together to form the **royal colony** of New Jersey. The proprietors had to give up their rights to the queen. Already the governor of New York, Cornbury also became New Jersey's royal governor in 1703.

Anne Stuart became queen in 1702.

22

At that time there were about 14,000 people in New Jersey, including Native Americans. In addition to the English and Dutch, there were settlers from Scotland, Sweden, and Finland. Many forms of religion were practiced, including Anglican, Puritan, Presbyterian, Lutheran, Baptist, and Quaker. Years earlier New Jersey had put a policy of religious freedom in place.

But the problems involving property ownership continued. It was reported that Lord Cornbury cared more for card games and money than carrying out Queen Anne's instructions. Rumors claimed he freely accepted bribes. He earned the reputation as the worst governor New Jersey ever had and was removed from office in 1709. In 1710 he returned to England in shame.

Colonial Anglicans gather outside after a church service.

royal colony—a colony controlled by a monarch or his representatives

After Cornbury returned to England, John Lovelace became governor of New York and New Jersey. In 1738 several **statesmen** argued successfully that New Jersey should have its own governor rather than share one with New York. One of these statesmen, Lewis Morris, became the first governor to serve only New Jersey.

Nothing seemed to solve the problems of who owned which property. A **riot** broke out in Newark in 1745. Similar incidents then occurred in Middlesex, Somerset, Morris, and Hunterdon Counties. Riots destroyed the jails. The government of New Jersey was proving to be ineffective.

New Jersey also faced economic problems. The colony imported more goods from England than it sold. Unwilling to force taxes on its people, New Jersey established a way for each county to borrow money. Still by 1765, New Jersey owed more money than any of the other colonies. Under British rule, though, the colony had the support to grow through trade and defense. But that would not last long since some colonists began to dislike British rule.

Did You Know?

Benjamin Franklin's son, William, served as the New Jersey Colony's last royal governor from 1762 to 1776.

Lewis Morris (1671–1746)

Lewis Morris was born in Morrisania, part of present-day Bronx, New York. He owned large estates in both New York and New Jersey. He became an important member of the East Jersey Board of Proprietors. He also acted as an agent for the West Jersey Society. He hoped to be the first royal governor of New Jersey but was angry when the position was given to Lord Cornbury. He took part in the actions to remove Cornbury as governor, speaking out about his bad behavior. In 1738 Morris became the first governor of New Jersey. As governor he strongly opposed bribery and **tyranny**. He served as governor until his death in 1746.

statesman—a person who helps the government with its decisions and business

riot—to act in a violent and often uncontrollable way

tyranny—a cruel or unfair government in which all power is in the hands of a single ruler

Chapter 5

Daily Life in the Jerseys

Early New Jersey settlers lived in log huts. Later the huts were replaced by one-story homes with one to three rooms. But over time more and more New Jersey colonists were building two-story homes of stone and brick with additional rooms.

Clothing was coarse, especially work clothes. Men wore breeches, buckled below the knee, and woolen stockings. Women wore long dresses. Children dressed like adults.

Women cooked stews over an open hearth. They made sausage, cheese, and butter at home. Most of the food came directly from a family's own farm and garden. The settlers grew grain such as wheat, corn, oats, barley, and rye. They also planted pumpkins, squash, and beans.

This New Jersey farmhouse was built in 1676.

Families owned animals to help them work the land and feed the family. A common occupation was farming, but there were also many weavers and people working in sawmills, **gristmills**, wool mills, and even small factories. Some women and girls did the weaving at home.

The Dutch brought slavery with them to New Jersey and engaged in the slave trade. East New Jersey, where the Dutch settled, depended highly on the work of slaves during the 1600s. There were fewer slaves in West New Jersey, where Quakers held antislavery beliefs and relied on immigrants for work.

Critical Thinking with Primary Sources

Absalom Bainbridge of Princeton owned a slave named Prime. Bainbridge sided with the British during the Revolutionary War. He fled New Jersey and took Prime with him to Brooklyn. But in 1778 Prime escaped and returned to Princeton. He believed in independence and joined the Continental army. Another man claimed Prime was his property during the war. The state of New Jersey fought against this, and Prime won his freedom in 1786. Prime wrote this letter asking for his freedom. Do you think the Revolutionary War helped Prime make his case to become a free man?

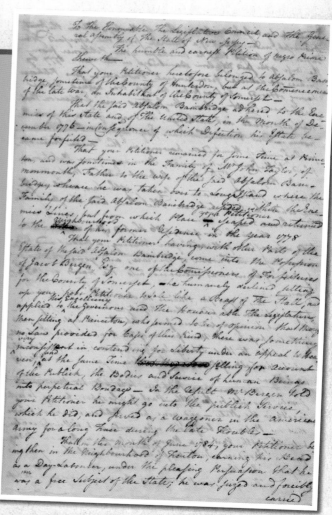

At School

Children often learned to read and write at home after dinner when their chores were done. Towns that had been settled by New Englanders, such as Newark, had a schoolhouse and a teacher.

New Jersey was the only colony to have two colleges. In 1746 John Witherspoon, a well-respected Presbyterian minister, founded the College of New Jersey, now known as Princeton University. Queen's College, now known as Rutgers University, was founded in New Brunswick in 1766.

John Witherspoon (1723–1794)

In 1768 at age 45 Reverend John Witherspoon arrived in America from Scotland to become president of the College of New Jersey in Princeton. He developed a reputation as a great leader who attracted students from many colonies. Among his students were a future president, James Madison, and a future vice president, Aaron Burr. Witherspoon supported the American Revolution. He served as a New Jersey **delegate** to the Continental Congress and was one of the signers of the Declaration of Independence.

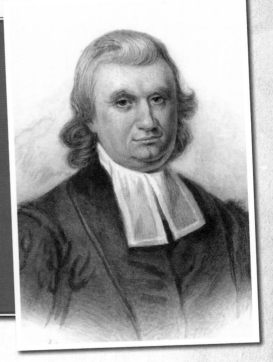

At Play

When their chores and learning were done, children could play with their toys. Dolls were made at home from corn husks and corncobs, wood, and rags. Toy animals made of wood, bone, nuts, shells, and sticks also kept children entertained.

This woodcut shows a Dutch family at home.

In the Community

People came together for many types of activities. Neighbors helped out when a man wanted to build a home or a farm. Other events included fairs, housewarmings, and quilting parties. They also held apple-butter and cornhusking competitions.

Churches provided opportunities for gathering too. Faith helped keep families and communities together. If religious groups couldn't afford to build a church, some services were held in houses or barns.

Did You Know?

New Jersey offered a lot of political and religious freedom. Because so many different types of settlers came to New Jersey for this freedom, the colony had one of the most mixed populations.

Chapter 6:
The Cockpit of the Revolution

While being under British rule helped New Jersey's economy for a time, not all colonists were happy with it. They did not like following the laws of a country across the ocean when they could not help make those laws. After its victory in the French and Indian War in 1763, the British began passing laws to help pay for the war. The colonists had to pay new taxes and new fees for goods coming from overseas, such as sugar, coffee, and tea. An especially unpopular law was the Stamp Act, which put a tax on paper items, such as newspapers. Protests against these laws led to the Revolutionary War.

Colonists protested the Stamp Act, believing Britain would ruin America with its laws.

During the Boston Tea Party, colonists dressed as Native Americans and threw crates of tea into Boston Harbor. The tea party in New Jersey followed Boston's example.

New Jersey's role in the American Revolution started with a protest over tea in 1774. It took place one year after the more famous Boston Tea Party. In the small town of Greenwich in Cumberland County, a group of about 40 men disguised themselves as Native Americans. They stormed a basement where a load of British tea had been stored. They took the tea and burned it. They would pay no tax on this tea.

Then the first shots of the Revolutionary War were fired at the battles of Lexington and Concord in Massachusetts on April 19, 1775. New Jersey's important location between New York and Philadelphia made it the site of nearly 300 major battles, raids, and skirmishes. No other colony saw more fighting. For this reason New Jersey earned the nickname "Cockpit of the Revolution."

The Battle of Trenton

In Trenton, New Jersey, on December 26, 1776, the Continental army faced off against **Hessian** troops fighting for Britain. The Hessians had taken the city of Trenton and were celebrating Christmas there. George Washington decided to lead the Continental army in a surprise attack.

On Christmas night, Washington and his soldiers crossed the dangerous, mostly frozen Delaware River to get to the city. By morning they attacked. Still tired from their holiday celebration the night before, the Hessians were quickly overtaken. Many escaped, but Washington's army took nearly 1,000 prisoners. Only four American soldiers were wounded, and two froze to death on the way to Trenton.

Washington's army beat the Hessians holding Trenton with few American losses.

The Battle of Princeton

The British were worried after the Americans won at the Battle of Trenton. On January 2, 1777, British General Charles Cornwallis took his army of 8,000 to Trenton to defeat Washington's 5,000 soldiers. But Washington knew he was outnumbered. So Washington and his army planned an escape. They left their fires burning and quietly snuck around the British camp and headed toward Princeton.

At dawn Washington's men encountered a small force of British troops who were on their way to Trenton. Outnumbered five to one, this small British band retreated within 15 minutes. In the Battle of Princeton, the British lost almost 300 soldiers, and the Americans lost around 40. The Continental army had succeeded in forcing the British out of most of southern New Jersey.

The War Leaves New Jersey

In the summer of 1778, 12,000 British troops marched through New Jersey. The Continental army hoped to cut them off before they could reach supplies in New York.

Commanding 5,000 of the Continental soldiers, Charles Lee met the British at Monmouth, New Jersey. However, Lee failed to give the officers specific orders, and their surprise attack turned into confusion. Lee ordered a retreat, and his troops ran back to Washington's main army as it came to attack from behind. When Washington saw their disorder and the British chasing them, he rallied his troops together to fight. They held out against the British, but the soldiers fought all day in extreme heat. The Battle of Monmouth was the longest single day of fighting during the entire war. However, the Continental army could not keep British troops from reaching New York City.

George Washington scolds Charles Lee for his failure before the Battle of Monmouth.

> *"On friday there was an Alarm our Milita was Calld; The Regelars come over into elesebeth town Where they had a Brush With a Small Party of our People; then marched Quietly up to Newark; & took all the Cattle they Could…"*
>
> —Jemima Condict, September 12, 1777, Pleasantdale, New Jersey

Soldiers endured severe heat the day of the Battle of Monmouth. Some soldiers died from the heat.

However, in June 1780, the British heard about a near **mutiny** of the Continental army in Morristown. Hoping to turn the situation into an easy victory, the British headed to Morristown to attack. This time, however, the Continental army managed to stop the 5,000 British troops at Springfield. The Continental army succeeded in keeping the British from reaching Morristown. The British retreated but burned Springfield homes and buildings along the way. The Battle of Springfield was the last major British invasion in New Jersey.

Washington spent about half his time during the Revolutionary War in New Jersey. Morristown served informally as the military capital of the Revolution. Washington found good viewpoints on high ground in the Watchung Mountains that allowed him to observe the British.

The Continental army also spent three winters in New Jersey, two of them at Morristown. One of these, the winter of 1779–1780, was the coldest of the century in that region. The winter of 1778–1779 was spent at Middlebrook. Their position was protected from the enemy at these locations due to the landscape of the Great Swamp and the mountains. And the watchful eyes of local **Patriots** also helped the army.

Washington's army builds its camp at Morristown during the harsh winter of 1779–1780.

An initial peace treaty ended the war in January 1783. Still, the Continental Congress moved from Philadelphia to Princeton, New Jersey, in June to ensure its own safety. Washington stayed at Princeton for 10 weeks and wrote his farewell address to his troops while in residence in nearby Rocky Hill. Princeton served as the national capital for four months that year. In November, Congress received news that the peace treaty had been signed. The Revolutionary War was over and Great Britain officially recognized the United States as an independent nation.

Patience (1725–1786) and Rachel Lovell (1735?–1796?), Sister Spies

As children in Bordentown, New Jersey, Patience and Rachel Lovell liked to mold bread dough into shapes and then color them with dyes. Patience and Rachel started a wax-sculpting business. During the Revolutionary War, Patience was living in England. As a well-known sculptor, she had access to highly important people. She **smuggled** messages about what she learned in the heads of the wax sculptures she sent to Rachel, who passed the messages on to the Continental Congress.

Patriot—a person who sided with the colonies during the Revolutionary War

smuggle—to secretly and illegally bring items into or out of an area

Chapter 7:
Becoming a State

After earning its independence, New Jersey, like the other colonies, had to learn how to govern itself. During the war the 13 Colonies had joined together, but they still wanted to create a single national government. While this government needed time to grow, New Jersey needed to recover from the war. Because so many battles took place there, New Jersey suffered greatly. Farms had been raided and ruined. Debt was staggering. New Jersey had to begin rebuilding. It was also a time to revisit old laws. In 1786, for example, the state legislature said there would be no more importing of slaves.

ARTICLES

Of Confederation and perpetual Union between the States of *New-Hampshire, Massachusetts-Bay, Rhode-Island* and *Providence Plantations, Connecticut, New-York, New-Jersey, Pennsylvania, Delaware, Maryland, Virginia, North-Carolina, South-Carolina* and *Georgia.*

ARTICLE I. THE Stile of this CONFEDERACY shall be "The UNITED STATES OF AMERICA.

ART. II. EACH State retains its sovereignty, freedom and independence, and every power, jurisdiction and right, which is not by this confederation expressly delegated to the United States, in Congress assembled.

ART. III. THE said states hereby severally enter into a firm league of friendship with each other, for their common defence, the security of their liberties, and their mutual and general welfare, binding themselves to assist each other, against all force offered to, or attacks made upon them, or any of them, on account of religion, sovereignty, trade, or any other pretence whatever.

ART. IV. The better to secure and perpetuate mutual friendship and intercourse among the people of the different states in this union, the free inhabitants of each of these states, paupers, vagabonds, and fugitives from justice excepted, shall be intitled to all priviledges and immunities of free citizens in the several states ; and the people of each state shall have free ingress and regress to and from any other state, and shall enjoy therein all the privileges of trade and commerce, subject to the same duties, impositions and restrictions as the inhabitants thereof respectively, provided that such restriction shall not extend so far as to prevent the removal of property imported into any state, to any other state of which the owner is an inhabitant ; provided also that no imposition, duties or restriction shall be laid by any state, on the prop

The Articles of Confederation were printed in 1777.

Not all states agreed with the 1777 Articles of Confederation that each colony was expected to follow. Some states, such as Virginia, wanted to put their own plans for the national government in place. The Virginia Plan stated that each state would be represented in the national government based on its population. But New Jersey was a small state, so it would have less power than larger states. When delegates gathered in Philadelphia in 1787 to draft a constitution for the new country, New Jersey pushed for the nation to use its Paterson Plan.

William Paterson (1745–1806)

Born in Ireland in 1745, William Paterson attended the College of New Jersey and became a lawyer. During the Revolutionary War, Paterson held several posts to promote the cause of the Patriots. He became attorney general of New Jersey in 1776. He was elected to the U.S. Senate and became the state of New Jersey's second governor in 1790. Later he served as an associate judge of the U.S. Supreme Court.

Put forth by New Jersey's William Paterson, the plan called for each state to have equal representation in the new national government, no matter how big or small the state. After some debate this led to the country's two government bodies. The Senate would have equal representation in each state, and the House of Representatives would be based on population. When New Jersey **ratified** the U.S. Constitution in 1787, it became the third state.

After business started growing again, New Jersey was well positioned to take a leading role in the new United States of America. As a center for industry, New Jersey helped shape the development of the nation.

Delegates create a new plan of government, the U.S. Constitution, at the Constitutional Convention in 1787.

> *"... there are reasons which strongly recommend the state of New Jersey for the purpose [of national industry]. It is thickly populated—provisions are there abundant and cheap."*
>
> —Alexander Hamilton, 1791

Did You Know?

Alexander Hamilton had a dream for national industry based in New Jersey. His plan helped to establish the town of Paterson, home of mills, iron foundries, and locomotive manufacturing.

Timeline

1609 Henry Hudson explores the Atlantic coast.

1624 The first Dutch colonists arrive in New Netherland.

1625 The Dutch West India Company establishes New Amsterdam, present-day New York City.

1630 The Dutch settle at Pavonia (Jersey City).

1638 Swedes establish the colony of New Sweden on the lower Delaware River.

1655 The Dutch take over New Sweden, and it becomes part of New Netherland.

1660 New Jersey's first village, Bergen, is founded.

1664 The Duke of York sends Richard Nicolls to take over New Netherland. The Duke of York also grants New Jersey land to Lord John Berkeley and Sir George Carteret.

1665–1667 Six New Jersey towns are founded: Elizabethtown, Middletown, Shrewsbury, Woodbridge, Piscataway, and Newark.

1672 War breaks out between England and the Netherlands.

1674 Berkeley sells half of New Jersey to Quakers.

1676 New Jersey splits into East Jersey and West Jersey.

1682 Twenty-four proprietors acquire East Jersey.

1702 Queen Anne sends Lord Cornbury to govern New York and New Jersey. The proprietors of East and West Jersey give up their powers of government to England. East and West Jersey unite as a royal colony.

1738 New Jersey has its own royal governor.

1746 The College of New Jersey (now called Princeton University) is founded.

1758 The Lenni Lenape reservation at Brotherton is established.

1766 Queen's College (now known as Rutgers University) is founded.

1774 The New Jersey Tea Party takes place in Cumberland County.

1775 The Revolutionary War begins with the Battles of Lexington and Concord in Massachusetts.

1776 The Battle of Trenton takes place in December.

1777 The Battle of Princeton takes place in January.

1778 The Battle of Monmouth takes place in June.

1779 The Battle of Paulus Hook (Jersey City) takes place in August.

1780 The Battle of Springfield takes place in June.

1783 The Continental Congress moves to Princeton. Washington writes a farewell address to his troops in Rocky Hill. A peace treaty with Britain is signed.

1787 New Jersey ratifies the U.S. Constitution and becomes the third state.

Glossary

colony (KAH-luh-nee)—a place that is settled by people from another country and is controlled by that country

delegate (DEL-uh-guht)—someone who represents other people at a meeting

gristmill (GRIST-mil)—a building for grinding grain

Hessian (HESH-uhn)—a German soldier, usually from the region of Hesse, hired by the British to fight in the Revolutionary War

hominy (HOHM-i-nee)—coarsely ground corn boiled in water

immigrant (IM-uh-gruhnt)—someone who settles permanently in another country

indigo (IN-duh-goh)—a plant that produces a deep-blue dye

longhouse (LAWNG-houss)—a long, narrow house usually for members of one clan

mutiny (MYOOT-uh-nee)—a rebellion of soldiers against their officers

Patriot (PAY-tree-uht)—a person who sided with the colonies during the Revolutionary War

patroon (pah-TROON)—a Dutch landholder in New Jersey or New York who was granted the land and certain rights in exchange for bringing 50 new settlers to the colony

plantation (plan-TAY-shuhn)—a large farm where crops are raised by people who live there

proprietor (proh-PREYE-uh-ter)—a person given ownership of a colony

Protestant (PROT-uh-stuhnt)—a Christian who does not belong to the Roman Catholic or the Orthodox Church

Puritan (PYOOR-uh-tuhn)—a member of a religious group that wanted simpler worship and stricter discipline in the Church of England

Quaker (KWAY-kur)—a member of the Religious Society of Friends, a group founded in the 1600s, that prefers simple religious services and opposes war

quitrent (KWIT-rent)—a fixed rent payable to a colony's leader

ratify (RAT-uh-fye)—to formally approve

reservation (rez-er-VAY-shuhn)—an area of land set aside for Native Americans

riot (RYE-uht)—to act in a violent and often uncontrollable way

royal colony (ROI-uhl KAH-luh-nee)—a colony controlled by a monarch or his representatives

smallpox (SMAWL-poks)—a disease that spreads easily from person to person, causing chills, fever, and pimples that scar

smuggle (SMUHG-uhl)—to secretly and illegally bring items into or out of an area

statesman (STATES-muhn)—a person who helps the government with its decisions and business

tyranny (TIHR-uh-nee)—a cruel or unfair government in which all power is in the hands of a single ruler

wigwam (WIG-whahm)—a round hut made of poles covered with bark, leaves, or animal skins

Critical Thinking Using the Common Core

1. What are some of the ways New Jersey stood out among the 13 Colonies? (Key Ideas and Details)
2. Examine the maps of Colonial New Jersey in Chapters 2 and 3. What similarities do you notice? What are some differences? (Integration of Knowledge and Ideas)
3. What words in the primary sources are unfamiliar to you? Can you determine their meanings from the text? (Craft and Structure)

Read More

Cunningham, Kevin. *The New Jersey Colony*. New York: Scholastic, 2011.

Misztal, Maggie. *The Colony of New Jersey*. New York: PowerKids Press, 2016.

Noble, Trinka Hakes and Jim Madsen. *The People of Twelve Thousand Winters*. Ann Arbor, Mich.: Sleeping Bear Press, 2012.

Internet Sites

FactHound offers a safe, fun way to find Internet sites related to this book. All of the sites on FactHound have been researched by our staff.

Here's all you do:
Visit *www.facthound.com*
Type in this code: 9781515722359

Super-cool stuff! Check out projects, games and lots more at **www.capstonekids.com**

Source Notes

Page 13, callout quote: Gabriel Thomas. *An Historical and Geographical Account of the Province and Country of Pensilvania and West-New-Jersey in America.* London: A. Baldwin, 1698. Accessed November 8, 2015. http://digital.library.pitt.edu/cgi-bin/t/text/text-idx?c=darltext;cc=darltext;view=toc;idno=31735056287646.

Page 21, callout quote: "The Lord Cornbury's Commission to be Governor of New-Jersey," in William A. Whitehead (ed.), *Documents Relating to the Colonial History of the State of New Jersey, Archives of the State of New Jersey, First Series, Vol. II, 1687–1703.* Newark: Daily Advertiser Printing House, 1881, p. 489.

Page 35, callout quote: Jemima Condict. *Jemima Condict, Her Book: Being a Transcript of the Diary of an Essex County Maid During the Revolutionary War.* Carteret Book Club, 1930, 66–67.

Page 41, callout quote: "Prospectus of the Society for Establishing Useful Manufactures, [August 1791]." Founders Online, National Archives. Source: *The Papers of Alexander Hamilton, vol. 9, August 1791–December 1791,* ed. Harold C. Syrett. New York: Columbia University Press, 1965, pp. 144–153. Accessed December 5, 2015. http://founders.archives.gov/documents/Hamilton/01-09-02-0114.

Regions of the 13 Colonies		
Northern Colonies	**Middle Colonies**	**Southern Colonies**
Connecticut, Massachusetts, New Hampshire, Rhode Island	Delaware, New Jersey, New York, Pennsylvania	Georgia, Maryland, North Carolina, South Carolina, Virginia
land more suitable for hunting than farming; trees cut down for lumber; trapped wild animals for their meat and fur; fished in rivers, lakes, and ocean	the "Breadbasket" colonies—rich farmland, perfect for growing wheat, corn, rye, and other grains	soil better for growing tobacco, rice, and indigo; crops grown on huge farms called plantations; landowners depended heavily on servants and slaves to work in the fields

Select Bibliography

Allinson, Samuel. "A Fragmentary History of the Delaware Indians in New Jersey," *Proceedings of New Jersey Historical Society*, Second Series, Vol. IV, 1875–1877. Newark: Daily Advertiser Offices, 1877. January 21, 1875. http://archive.org/stream/proceedingsofnew04newj/proceedingsofnew04newj_djvu.txt.

"Brotherton & Weekping Indian Communities of NJ: Primary Documents Related to Brotherton Indians," from the Foster Collection. http://brotherton-weekping.tripod.com/id19.html.

Condict, Jemima. *Jemima Condict, Her Book: Being a Transcript of the Diary of an Essex County Maid During the Revolutionary War*. Newark, N.J.: Carteret Book Club, 1930.

Green, Howard L., ed. *Words That Make New Jersey History: A Primary Source Reader*, Expanded Edition. New Brunswick, N.J.: Rivergate/Rutgers University Press, 2009.

"Instructions from Queen Anne to Lord Cornbury as Governor of New Jersey," in William A. Whitehead (ed.), *Documents Relating to the Colonial History of the State of New Jersey, Archives of the State of New Jersey, First Series, Vol. II, 1687–1703*. Newark: Daily Advertiser Printing House, 1881.

"The Lord Cornbury's Commission to be Governor of New-Jersey," in William A. Whitehead (ed.), *Documents Relating to the Colonial History of the State of New Jersey, Archives of the State of New Jersey, First Series, Vol. II, 1687–1703*. Newark: Daily Advertiser Printing House, 1881.

Lurie, Maxine N., ed. *A New Jersey Anthology*, Second Edition. New Brunswick, N.J.: Rivergate/Rutgers University Press, 2010.

McCormick, Richard P. *New Jersey from Colony to State, 1609–1789*. New Brunswick, N.J.: Rutgers University Press, 1964.

Middleton, Richard and Anne Lombard. *Colonial America: A History to 1763*. Malden, Mass.: Wiley-Blackwell, 2011.

Stansfield, Charles A., Jr. *A Geography of New Jersey: The City in the Garden*, Second Edition. New Brunswick, N.J.: Rutgers University Press, 1998.

Thomas, Gabriel. *An Historical and Geographical Account of the Province and Country of Pennsilvania and West-New-Jersey in America*. London: A. Baldwin, 1698. http://digital.library.pitt.edu/cgi-bin/t/text/text-idx?c=darltext;cc=darltext;view=toc;idno=31735056287646

Weiss, Harry B. *Life in Early New Jersey*. Princeton, N.J.: Van Nostrand, 1964.

Weslager, C. A. *The Delaware Indians: A History*. New Brunswick, N.J.: Rutgers University Press, 1972.

Worth-Baker, Marcia. "Witness to History: Diary of a Revolution." NJmonthly.com. June 27, 2014. http://njmonthly.com/articles/jersey-living/witness-to-history-diary-revolution/.

Index